Memoir by
Elsa Lanchester

SONGS BY FORMAN BROWN

Introduction by Ray Bradbury

CAPRA PRESS
Santa Barbara/1988

Cover design by Francine Rudesill.
Design and typography by Jim Cook (Santa Barbara, California)

LIBRARY OF CONGRESS CATALOGING-IN-PUBLICATION DATA

Lanchester, Elsa, 1902–1985
    Gamut of girls / by Elsa Lanchester; lyrics by Forman Brown.
    ISBN 0-88496-292-X (pbk.) : $8.95
    1. Brown, Forman George—Appreciation 2. Lanchester, Elsa, 1902-1985.
    3. Turnabout Players. 4. Humorous poetry, American. 5. Humorous songs—Texts.
    6. Women—Poetry. I. Brown, Forman George. II. Title.
PS3503.R812Z77   1988   88-15439
611'.54—dc19   CIP

Published by CAPRA PRESS
Post Office Box 2068
Santa Barbara, California 93120

□ Contents

□ Foreword

The verses in this collection were written for Elsa Lanchester, who performed them at Hollywood's Turnabout Theatre. A few of the verses are serious, but most are, or are intended to be, funny. Their author, however, cheerfully acknowledges that they are not as serious or as funny on the printed page as they were in the pixie presentations of Miss Lanchester, so to the memory of this amazingly versatile artist they are dedicated— "A Gamut of Girls."

—*Forman Brown*

☐ Elsa's Story:
What *else* but *Elsa*?!

What is there to say, this late in time, about Elsa Lanchester and her full life at the Turnabout Theatre? To start with, the Turnabout Theatre and Elsa launched themselves on an unsuspecting public during the very years when I was trying valiantly to do the same. I was in my very early twenties, making fifteen dollars a week at writing, when I was lucky, and as soon as I had a few dollars saved up, I arrived at their performance.

I was hooked. No, that's not strong enough. I fell completely in love with the theater, the way it was built, the way it was written, and the grand way in which it was acted. At the time, I didn't realize that one day all of these people would be friends. As the years passed, I attended the Turnabout some thirty to forty times, dragging friends and relatives along for the collision.

Not only did I love what I saw on the stage, but I got warm encouragement from the Turnabouters, who not only acted but appeared in the box office selling tickets on the dozens of occasions when I showed up with my hard-earned cash. They seemed to enjoy the news when I told them I was moving up into life, with more and more stories and more and more attention. Meanwhile, their theater and its audiences grew.

In later years, I got to know Elsa well. One afternoon in 1956, she and Charles Laughton showed up at our small tract house near Westwood Boulevard in Los Angeles. My wife Maggie and I welcomed them in to meet our two daughters, Susan and Ramona.

Charlie stood over Ramona and, laughing down at her, jiggling his jowls, shouted: "Aren't I *fat*!?"

I took the daughters over to swim at Elsa's and Charlie's on numerous occasions, and in that time, reminisced about the Turnabout and how sad was the last night when it shut down forever.

I tried my hand at writing a small science-fiction operetta for Elsa but, let's face it, I was no Forman Brown. Writing such deceptively simply lyrics takes a very special talent. I went back to my short stories and novels.

And now, many years on, I have here a chance to repay an old debt, to say once again how special were those nights and how dear those performers. This book cannot possibly capture the warm quality of those occasions, of course. But it is a needful record. And I am proud and pleased to be here up front to call to Elsa's dear ghost and Forman's living spirit: *"Begin!"*

—Ray Bradbury
January 14, 1988

□ The Memoir

"How did you ever start doing songs?" was a common question I was often asked at Turnabout. Different people have passions for collecting different things—paintings or old books, china dogs, butterflies, love affairs, etchings. I always had a passion for collecting songs. All sorts of songs.

When I was just five or six I was an intense little girl who took to picking up songs as a duck takes to water. My parents took me to the English seaside towns of Clacton-on-Sea or Brighton for our summer holidays. At all seaside towns there would be a little wooden stage erected on the beach, and a show performed by a Pierrot or maybe a clown, but always a red-nosed comic. After a short show children were invited to come up from the audience and compete in singing the songs they had just heard—at least the choruses. Sometimes they sang them balancing on a barrel, winning higher prizes and louder applause. I was too frightened to get up on the stage, but I soon picked up all the songs and sang them at home to myself.

> He pushed me into the parlor,
> pushed the parlor door;
> pushed himself upon my knee,
> pushed his face in front of me.
> He pushed me round to the jeweler
> near the Hippodrome,
> then he pushed me in front of the clergyman
> and then he pushed me home!

My parents were always a bit arty. They were "advanced." They supported pacifism, vegetarianism, socialism, atheism, and all that. (My mother was a suffragette, of course.) I made my own sandals, did hand-weaving, studied violin, Dalcroze eurhythmics, classical dancing, and had singing lessons. In singing class I studied with seven or eight little girls. I still remember one or two ghastly songs from that time:

> Marjorie, Marjorie
> dancing in the sun,
> in and out of the house is she
> teasing everyone.
> Rosy cheeks fair to see,
> laughing eyes of blue;
> Marjorie, Marjorie,
> all our love's for you.
>
> Oh, oh, little Yo-San
> with your face of tan
> and your dear little eyes
> peeping over your fan . . .
> Yo-o-San!

With Oriental gestures. At the time I thought I was wildly graceful.

At ten my mother met Raymond Duncan, who thought I was talented and eventually sent me to Paris to study dancing with his sister Isadora. As one of the Raymond Duncan group I learned many folk songs. I remember one, "The Bitter Withy," a delightful story about Jesus Christ being whipped by his mother for killing three men.

At Isadora's Dancing Academy, I learned a song called "Un Bon Mouvement" from a phonograph record. It was about cabbages. In England, babies are supposed to emerge from under gooseberry bushes. In America, the stork is supposed to bring them. But in France, they are said to come from cabbages. "Un Bon Mouvement" told about the thirty-two ways of planting cabbages.

In the next few years I collected dozens of songs wherever I could. One of my favorites was "The Raggle-Taggle Gypsies-O!"—perhaps my first adventure into sex—about a rich lady who ran away to become a "hippie."

> Oh, what care I for my goosefeather bed
> with the sheets turned down so bravely-o?
> Tonight I'll sleep in a cold, open field
> along with the raggle-taggle gypsies-o!

Springing out of this free and Bohemian life, six years later I started a nightclub with a group of friends. (That's not really as bad as it sounds.) We couldn't get a liquor license so we couldn't make any money. We rented a dreary old warehouse, fixed it up; painted the walls pink, the woodwork yellow, and put up red velvet curtains—and all candlelight. We called this lovely firetrap The Cave of Harmony. We put on one-act plays by Chekhov, Pirandello, and others. If occasionally an actor couldn't show up, that's when I got up and sang a song—doing bits and pieces from anywhere.

> The best landlady you can find
> is a nice little wife of your own.
> She won't take your sugar or your tea,
> won't be afraid to sit upon your knee.
> Find a nice little sweetheart
> and change her name to Brown,
> then with your landlady just settle up
> and then settle down.

At first I dressed myself in crepe paper costumes, and eventually I became a part of the program and learned more songs. Once, when I was arranging props for a play and had a duster in my hand, the audience started to applaud, and so that stayed in. My earliest charwoman. As we began putting together more cabaret shows, I began unearthing more old songs that would be new.

> Cock-a doodle, cock-a-doodle,
> I'm the cock of the north!
> Chase me, Charlie!
> over the barley,
> I lost the leg of my drawers;
> if you find it
> wash and iron it,
> give it to one of the boys!

"The Ratcatcher's Daughter," a mid-nineteenth century song,

served me all through the years. It was one of the many songs I found in the British Museum, and I did it first at The Cave of Harmony.

At The Cave we had a little dance band, and served club sandwiches, eggs and kippers. When the dancing stopped, people sat on the floor to watch the show. The Cave of Harmony went on for four years. A lot of famous people started dropping in at our cabaret. H.G. Wells, Aldous Huxley, Arnold Bennett, Evelyn Waugh, and other writers, poets, painters, and musicians. Sometimes a song or a poem was written for me to perform.

> I may be fast,
> I may be loose,
> I may be easy to seduce!

Eventually I was singing in a West End revue and working in a nightspot after the show. The revue was *Riverside Nights* and the nightspot was The Midnight Follies (at the Metropole Hôtel). Changing costumes in a taxi going from one show to the other, the taxi was stopped one night by a policeman who wondered what was going on behind the temporarily covered windows. It was me changing from "Please Sell No More Drink To My Father" (black cotton stockings, Victorian middy blouse, etc.) to Nell Gwynne (and her busty bodice). No crepe paper costumes anymore, but velvets and silks. Once again I did "The Ratcatcher's Daughter," but this time beautifully costumed by the English designer, John Armstrong. I was delighted with a wreath of little roses he made for me, and still have them.

In *The Midnight Follies*, A.P. Herbert wrote me a number called "Spare A Copper For The Lucky Baby." I was a glamorous gypsy on Derby Day wearing a rather grand satin patchwork shawl and holding a baby-bundle in my arms.

> Spare a copper for the lucky baby
> and a blessing shall be your reward.
> She's a regular fairy,
> brought luck to Queen Mary,
> health and wealth to the motherless lord
> who sent the kind stork

to the Duchess of York
and cured our dear Prince of his pain.
Well, you ask the Prince
if he's had the croup since—
he was good to Elizabeth Jane.

The Prince referred to was the then Prince of Wales, later the King and *later* the late Duke of Windsor. He was offended by the reference to his family and walked out, saying as he left: "This is very unusual!" The manager of the Metropole said: "We can't afford to offend a good customer."

I got the sack.

Then I began to act in plays, and it was at this time that I met Charles (Charles Laughton, that is). We met in a play called *Mr. Prohack* by Arnold Bennett. Charles and I were married in about a year and soon after left for America to appear in another play, *Payment Deferred.* I played his twelve-year-old daughter.

By this time, my singing had stopped totally. Until . . .

In 1941, I was having lunch with Helen Deutsch, the writer, in a restaurant on Sunset Strip, and she said that there were three guys she knew (I think she said "crazy guys") opening a little theater down on La Cienega Boulevard. She thought it would be a good place for me to get up and try out my old collection of songs.

Just like that.

So after lunch we dropped in to see what the place was like. The patio was a pile of rubble and the theater smelled of new wood and not yet of paint. The "three guys" and I talked for a few minutes. They all seemed to like the idea of my appearing, so without any fuss on either side I started to rehearse my numbers—of course, none of them written by Forman at this time. I sang three songs when I opened at the Turnabout. The first number was by A.P. Herbert: "He Didn't Oughter (Come To Bed In Boots)." Another charwoman. The next song was "The Ratcatcher's Daughter." The last was "Somebody Broke Lola's Saucepan." Three characterizations—each in a different costume—and this was to remain the pattern we used over the years.

The whole Turnabout idea was thought up and carried out by the Yale Puppeteers. It was the fulfillment of a wish to have their own theater after having toured America for years. Brandon, Burnett, and Brown—or "The Three B's" as they called themselves—were joined by Dorothy Neumann in their project. Then I came into the picture. With my old songs, new songs, pretty songs, wicked songs.

I joined the company at the beginning of their *third* week, after making a lot of excuses about not wanting to interfere with their original plan. Also, Charles had the idea that the Turnabouters would get one batch of publicity on their own publicized opening and then another batch when I joined them two weeks later.

I had wanted to do this kind of work again for so long and had not found the opportunity. Now when the opportunity came, I was too scared to get up and do my songs in front of the Hollywood celebrities who would be coming on opening night. I was so nervous, in fact, I wouldn't let Charles come to see me for weeks. When he finally did come, he brought Deanna Durbin, and I more or less lost my voice from sheer terror.

After being at Turnabout a short while I rather tentatively asked what their policy was. After all, I was a guest artist and a self-invited one at that. I did not know if I was wanted, and they on their part were not sure they should ask me to stay. So this roundabout series of conversations about their "policy" started. I twisted myself into knots and so did they. The trouble was the Yale Puppeteers didn't have a policy and never had one. They all looked dreadfully worried at the prospect of acquiring one.

Well, I stayed . . . and stayed and stayed.

Ultimately, the "policy" at the Turnabout was to change the material as often as Forman could produce it. And he produced a lot. After a whole year that had been to a great extent experimental, we had reduced all the best material to three complete and different shows. We played one each week, and in that way audiences could be sure of seeing something new and could come back sooner. And they did.

Financially the venture was successful, although the results might not have satisfied some people. It all depends on whether you want to earn a living or make lots of money. Although I was called the "guest artist," it was rather a joke after a whole year. Since I did not

16

take a salary, it gave me the freedom to come and go as needed. And the Yale Puppeteers no doubt liked it that way, too.

We never knew for sure why the Turnabout was such a success. We often used to sit around after the show and have coffee and cake and discuss the whole thing. Dorothy thought this and Forman thought that, and all of us dreamed where it might all lead. We were a bunch of people able to entertain an audience with the same relish that talented members of a family would get out of entertaining friends at a party. As we were getting to know ourselves in relationship to our audiences, so Forman was getting to know us. And this mutual sharpening of wits was, I believe, what was selling seats.

I knew that Forman had written all the puppet shows and all the songs for the other performers, and I waited expectantly for my first song. And I think the first song was "If You Can't Get In The Corners." It was about a charwoman. I did it with a duster in my hand. (Remember The Cave of Harmony?)

Over the years Forman wrote fifty or sixty songs for me. During all my time at the Turnabout Theatre as guest artist, my appearances in each of the several revues consisted of three solo spots, and that is why the songs in this collection are arranged in groups of three. I appeared in the first spot, the last spot, and a middle spot.

As a performer known principally as a film personality, I hoped first of all to avoid the conventional movie-star image. So my first appearance on the stage I wanted to look unlike an actress trying to look more glamorous than she is. I became, for example, the charwoman, a kitchen slavey, a frowzy housewife, or a slum brat. In short, a collection of distinctly unglamorous females. Since I was an actress, my second number was usually a ballad. Here I told a story and created, in song and dance, a picturesque character. As the ballads were usually period pieces, they gave me a chance to move about the stage in colorful costumes. So now, having shown myself looking my worst and best, for my last number I could be as outrageous as I chose: potentates' mistresses, ladies of the night and all that goes with them, and that sort of thing.

Whenever Forman came up with a new number, it was immediately understood by both of us that it was destined for spot number one, number two, or number three. Charles said once that Forman and I made a true artistic marriage of talents and a happy one. As he usually was in such matters, I think he was right.

When Forman first played and sang a new number for me at the piano, I rarely reacted. It must have been rather discouraging for him, but I was already getting my first vision of who this character in the song was—and first thoughts should never be dismissed. If there is such a thing as inspiration, this first impression stays uppermost with you. You add, discard, and change; but rarely dismiss.

Stuffing Forman's song into my bag, I couldn't wait to get home. Then I'd get to my room and read the actual words carefully, and then sleep on them. Later I'd start to appreciate Forman's actual lines. I then roughly learned the tune on the piano with one finger.

In the privacy of my room, mostly late at night, I moved into the frame of an imaginary proscenium arch and then started working out the movements for telling the story. Pointing up jokes and double meanings with calculated looks. With regard to double meanings *(double entendres)* Forman was a specialist, but I sometimes topped him. He would often say at an early rehearsal: "How *could* you think I meant *that!*"

The art of selling the *double entendre* is to make the members of an audience feel almost guilty that such strange thoughts should pass through their minds. I am told that my innocent expression prior to my knowing smile is my number-one weapon. I had plenty of time to polish and sharpen this weapon at Turnabout.

The choreography of the hands and eyes and the directions you move in must be geometrically precise in order to create, as it were, a "map"—something on which to build the place and the person. A river, for example, can be made to exist. Look at the same spot for your river, think of willows and maybe rushes, gesture once or twice toward it—but not *on* the word "river." Before or after, but never on the word. This is a trap that often makes amateurs comical and inept in their roles.

My vision of the costumes started immediately with the framing of the movements. But in combing through the acres of clothes at Western Costume, the largest costumers in Hollywood, I often had to change the action of the song to fit the costume. Sometimes for the better. Often the costume came first, and Forman wrote for the costume. For instance, in the song "I'm Glad To See You're Back— (Your Back!)"—this costume was an original Worth model, a gift, and it was too small for me; so I just left the lacing at the back undone. Hence the song. Charles thought of the title, and Forman wrote it.

In the thirties, someone left me yards of black lace threaded with mauve ribbons on a voluminous tea-colored petticoat. This was made into a grand first-night evening gown by Victor Stiebel (who also dressed Princess Margaret) in London. This dress served as the outfit for "When A Lady Has A Piazza"—and how! Over the years of wear and tear I had it copied three times. So the right dress for the right song.

Bertolt Brecht made a comment about my work that I'd like to repeat. I know it is rather vain of me to recall a compliment. But to be understood is the greatest pleasure that a performer can experience. Brecht said that I was the only person he had seen who filled in the frame in the same way that the Japanese did in their prints. I was enchanted with this observation. I truly feel that a performer should be able to stand even in one corner of the stage and create rivers, houses, patios, lawns, laundromats, backyards, or whatever, without benefit of scenery or props. An example of this is a story of a stage manager at the Turnabout. He nearly had a fit by showtime on his first day at work. He had seen the show from the front, and now he couldn't find the lattice-work with the yellow roses for my "Gazebo" song. I used no lattice, let alone yellow roses.

Forman and I were never at cross purposes when it came to building a song. There was one general rule I did urge him to keep. And this rule I learned myself only by trial and error. The songs should have upbeat endings. My ladies in our songs all had to like their lives and be successful in the end. Forman, writer and poet, occasionally used to indulge in the sorrowful picturesqueness, for example, of a woman sitting by candlelight and ruminating about days gone by, and other such sad endings. I felt I didn't want to leave the audience in a downbeat mood. Certainly not at Turnabout.

Forman's upbeat endings were among his best inventions. As in

"Melinda Mame" and "Delphinia," Melinda "rode in a barouche with four white horses," and Delphinia "was done up in pink and was having a drink with a couple of men at the Stork." "My Man Is Riding In The Moonlight" is, I think, Forman's loveliest verse written for me at Turnabout. Such a beautiful piece of writing is above being upbeat or downbeat. It is the purely emotional surge that raises the spirits high in this number. I do not consider I did Forman justice in this case. Perhaps a better voice and a more earthy woman would have brought out its haunting qualities.

Nobody has a life plan that works exactly as one expects it to. But I must say, looking back, there is a pattern of parallels for me. "How did you ever start doing songs?" was a common question. But now it seems quite clear to me that I always was on the same track, a track that finally led to the Turnabout Theatre. The seaside shows, my early folk songs, the days at The Cave of Harmony, the cabarets, the nightspots, and the revue *Riverside Nights* (my slaveys, my stories, and my sirens)—all contributing to my performances on La Cienega Boulevard in Los Angeles.

I went to Turnabout for two weeks and stayed ten years.

And those years at Turnabout were truly growing years. And I literally *did* grow. I grew half an inch and my rib expansion gained two inches. The nightly workout, the singing and dancing, was as healthy as going to a gymnasium. What more could a person want? I had a second life, professional happiness, and friends backstage and friends in the audience, with time for films, and a life with Charles.

—*Elsa Lanchester*

□ Forman's Songs

IF YOU CAN'T GET IN THE CORNERS

Whenever I go to get a job, or have an interview,
the ladies always use the same manoeuvres:
They tell me how short my hours will be, how little I'll have to do
with their Electroluxes and their Hoovers.
That's when I fix 'em with my coldest gaze
and tell them what my husband, Egbert, says:

If you can't get in the corners, you might as well give up—
that's what he maintains.
No matter how you rig it you can never trust a spiggot,
he explains.
Why get tangled with a light-cord or a bloomin', billowin' bag
when all you need is a bit of spit and your finger and a rag?
O I hate a thing that whizzes and goes "slup-slup"—
if you can't get in the corners, you might as well give up!

Now Egbert, he used to sell them vacu-ums from door to door—
I met him when he came to demonstrate.
He put on such a pretty act there on the parlor floor
we fell in love, and soon he was my mate.
But Egbert changed his tactics then and there:
He said "You can put them devices—you know where?"

If you can't get in the corners, you may as well give up,
and me, I do agree.
A thing that sucks and blows through a nozzle or a hose
just ain't for me.
They're inventions of the devil, with their wheezin' and their hum:
Give me a piece of cheesecloth—you can keep your vacu-um!
One might do well enough for getting fleas off from a pup,
but if you can't get in the corners, you might as well give up.

I have a friend, a Mrs. Grimes, who hires out by the hour.
I tried to warn her, but she only sneered.
This house had got a new vacu-um—when she plugged in the
 power
one Whoosh!—her combinations disappeared!
As Mrs. Grimes remarked that night, her underwear was clean,
but what un-nerved her was havin' it snatched off—by a
 MACHINE!

If you can't get in the corners, you might as well give up—
it's elbow grease you need.
That horrid vulgar noise, it quite destroys your poise,
it does, indeed!

If Mother Nature hadn't giv'n us fingers, yes, and thumbs,
there might perhaps be some excuse for usin' vacu-ums.
But just like Egbert said when Maisie sent that moustache-cup:
If you can't get in the corners, you might as well give up.

I SHOULDN'T HAVE GONE TO THAT MATINEE

They were playing "East Lynne" at the Empire
and I wanted to see "East Lynne."
But Mother was busy, and Auntie was busy,
and Letty in sewing was up to her chin.
So I thought I would flout all conventions
and go to the Empire alone.
How could I foresee what would happen to me?
I'd never have gone had I known!

> I shouldn't have gone to that matinee,
> that Saturday matinee.
> My mother, she warned me to stay away
> from that Saturday matinee.

I'd a seat in the box at the Empire
with a vacant one at my side.
They'd started "East Lynne" when a fellow came in
and whispered, "Please, Miss, is this chair occupied?"
Well, I couldn't say "Yes" with conviction
so I said what he took to be "No."
He shoved in so tight that try as I might
I could not concentrate on the show.

> I shouldn't have gone to that matinee
> that Saturday matinee.
> My mother warned me to stay away
> from that Saturday matinee.

He shoved his chair closer and closer;
he couldn't control his hands.
I frowned, I was rude, but he misunderstood
and I'm awfully afraid he still misunderstands.
At first it was "Pardon me, please, Miss."

26

By the end of the act it was "Dear"!
Well! I really can't say what occurred in the play—
it might have been "Hamlet" or "Lear"!

> I shouldn't have gone to that matinee,
> that Saturday matinee.
> My mother she warned me to stay away
> from that Saturday matinee.

It might never have been so disastrous
had the episode stopped with "East Lynne,"
but it's hard to resist when a man will insist
on sending you roses, and sweets by the tin!
My family thinks—heaven knows what!
I daren't reveal how we met.
O, it's hard to pretend when you know, in the end,
what he wants he is certain to get!

> No, I shouldn't have gone to that matinee,
> that Saturday matinee.
> Though I can't quite forget it, I still can't regret it,
> that Saturday matinee.

THE MAHARANEE OF SWAT

Somewhere east of Punjab
lies the little state of Swat
where the elephants wear golden pants
and the weather is always hot.
There in her ivory palace
the Maharanee rules
while around her couch her ministers crouch
on seventeen silver stools.
But the Maharanee is fretful,
for not a mate can she get.
She is feeling so tête-a-tête-ful
but there's no one to tête-a-tête.
All the Princes seem to be taken—
they're a much too popular lot—
and the Maharanee can't find one Johnnie
to be Mahrajah of Swat.

O the Maharanee of Swat
she is in a difficult spot:
No Tom, Dick or Harry can ever marry
a Maharanee of Swat.

The lady's richer than Croesus,
she's a most expensive dame,
and she and her girls use rubies and pearls
in the royal pin-ball game.
Her Cadillac's platinum-plated;
she glitters when she goes out,
and her bracelets clank like the National Bank
whenever she moves about.
Her diamonds are big as gumdrops;

I have had the pleasure of meeting only one real Maharenee in my life, and she was not at all, I found to my considerable disappointment, like the Maharanee of Swat.

she drinks from an emerald cup,
and whenever she lets a crumb drop
there's a flunky to pick it up.
She counts her jewels by the barrel,
but in spite of all she's got
she can't locate a suitable mate
to be Maharajah of Swat.

O the Maharanee of Swat,
how ironical is her lot!
No interloper can hope to rope 'er,
the Maharanee of Swat.

Her ministers tried to sell her
the Pasha of Baleek,
but at eighty-three he seemed to be
a little bit antique.
Likewise the Prince of Poona
was available, she was told.
He was awfully cute in his Eton suit,
but only nine years old.
The Sultan of Lahore came,
but she squelched the Sultan flat.
You can hardly blame a respectable dame
for declining a name like that!
No wonder she got discouraged,
for it's not an enviable fate
to be Maharanee with all that money
and still no sight of a mate.

O the Maharanee of Swat
in spite of all that she's got,
her royal stature can't seem to catch her
a Maharajah of Swat.

Lately she has decided
on a rather daring move.
She figures since she can't get a prince
that her ministers approve,
she'll send across the ocean
where the picking should be good
and see if she can not get a man
who's a star in Hollywood.
He'd be an inspiration,
and his profile, like as not,
would cause a mild sensation
on the postage stamps of Swat.
Though her Grand Vizier is protesting
she looks him in the eye
and says "My man, if Aly Khan
than why on earth can't I?"

O the Maharanee of Swat
has hatched a wonderful plot,
but her latest script needs a hero shipped
from a motion picture lot.

A sample came on approval,
and the sample looked fine
she called "Okay, the man can stay.
From now on he'll be mine."
She dressed him in pale pink jodhpurs
and a turban of tiger fur,
and she positively felt as though she'd melt
whenever he looked at her.
He was very ornamental—
they made a handsome pair,
for his smile was O so dental
and Metro-Goldwyn-Mayer.

Her English is rather sketchy
but she's learned enough to know
for satisfaction to whisper "Action!
Camera! Lights! Let's go!"

O the Maharanee of Swat,
just see what her industry got!
She kept her chin up, and got a pin-up
for Maharajah of Swat!

THE HATPIN

My Granny was a very shrewd old lady,
the smartest woman that I ever met.
She used to say, "Now listen to me, Sadie,
there's one thing that you never must forget!"

"Never go walking without your hatpin—
the Law won't let you carry more than that.
For if you go walking out without your hatpin
you may lose your head as well as lose your hat!"

My Granny said men never could be trusted
no matter how refined they might appear.
She said that many a maiden's heart got busted
because men never had but one idear.
I've heard that Granpa really was a mess,
so Granny knew whereof she spoke, I guess.

Never go walking out without your hatpin,
not even to some very classy joint,
for when a fellow sees you've got a hatpin
he's very much more apt to get the point.

My Mama too set quite a bad example;
she never heeded Grandmama's advice.
She found that if you give a man a sample
the sample, somehow, never will suffice.
In fact it's rumored I might not have been
had Mama not gone out without her pin!

Never go walking out without your hatpin!
It's about the best protection you have got.
For if you go walking without your hatpin
you may come home without your you-know-what!

I suppose most of us have had the familiar experience of driving through a strange city and being particularly attracted by a certain building, and wondering what might be the story behind its walls. The following song tells what went on behind certain walls in a small city I once knew in the middle west. It is more or less a true story—the story of a lady whom we have called Melinda Mame.

MELINDA MAME

Jeremiah Bowers, the richest man in town,
he was the meanest man too.
He was hard as nails, and they still tell tales
of the bitter things he used to do.
Jeremiah Bowers, he owned the bank,
the drugstore and hotel,
and what he owned, and how he loaned,
people loved to tell.
Everybody hated Jeremiah,
everybody cursed his name.
Everyone allowed he was stiff and proud
except Melinda Mame.
Nobody trusted Jeremiah;
everybody felt the same.
Everybody said he'd be better dead
excepting Melinda Mame.

She lived over Bowers' drugstore—
dressmaking was her line.
Her fingers were nimble with needle and thimble
and her seams were straight and fine.

Everybody feared Jeremiah,
and everybody envied his game.
Everyone was sure he was past all cure
excepting Melinda Mame.
When he was forty Jeremiah married.
Everybody in the county came
to see him and his bride walking side by side—
excepting Melinda Mame.
The bride was twenty-two, and quite a beauty.

Everybody said it was a shame:
prophesied he'd beat her and mistreat her,
excepting Melinda Mame.

Rumour got around that evenings
when he would leave the store
he'd look at her window to see if Melinda
would beckon him to her door.

Everybody said it was a caution
said it was a sin and shame.
Everybody vowed it should not be allowed
excepting Melinda Mame.
At sixty, Jeremiah took pneumonia—
the doctor and the lawyer came,
and no one really cared, or hoped that he'd be spared,
excepting Melinda Mame.
The funeral at the church was quite impressive—
even the governor came.
And everyone tried to get inside
excepting Melinda Mame.

The procession was the longest one on record:
four cars to take the flowers,
and everybody read what they'd carved above his head:
"Here lies Jeremiah Bowers."

Then everybody went about his business
and everybody made a little game
of trying to figure who his money might go to—
excepting Melinda Mame.
His widow locked the house and went to Texas.
Everybody said it was a shame.
It was too big to be sold, everybody seemed to hold
excepting Melinda Mame.

A decorator fellow from St. Louis
with carloads of new furniture came,
and everyone thought it was some millionaire who'd bought it,
excepting Melinda Mame.

One night she left her room above the drugstore
and moved into the mansion on the hill,
and on the first of May she gave a big soiree
which people are discussing still.

She rides in a barouche with four white horses
and a footman with a fancy name,
and down beneath the clover Jeremiah's turned plumb over—
everybody says the same—
excepting—Melinda Mame!

We heard a good deal in the days when the following song was written about the Good Neighbor Policy. The song, although it does have no particular geographical setting, does have some bearing on the Good Neighbor Policy—but only, I think, in a domestic sense.

WHEN A LADY HAS A PIAZZA

Every night when the sun goes down
on my little white house on the edge of town
I sit on my porch and rock.
My neighbor on the left is Mrs. McFaul—
she never speaks to me at all—
she's in bed by nine o'clock.
Mrs. Partington lives on the other side,
she's a righteous woman with a military stride
and she ignores me too.
But Mr. Partington and Mr. McFaul
have both dropped in rather late to call,
a neighborly thing to do.

When a lady has a piazza
she has a prize indeed.
She can look on her piazza
as a friend in need.
For a girl who has a piazza
has a place on which to sit,
and people know a piazza
has a house attached to it.

Queenie bought rings and a yellow fox coat;
Nellie took a trip on a round-the-world boat,
but I bought a place to stay.
Queenie's looking the worse for wear
and Nellie—well, Nellie is God knows where,
but me, I'm doing okay.
I keep my kitchen slick and clean,
I starch my aprons and paint my screen
like my two neighbors do.

So I guess it's okay when the sun goes down
if I put on my lace and taffeta gown
and rock for an hour or two.

When a lady has a piazza she has a prize indeed.
She can look on her piazza as a friend in need.
For a girl who has a piazza has a place on which to sit,
and people know a piazza has a house attached to it.

Domesticity suits me fine
though I'd never have thought it was just my line
it seems to agree with me.
When you've got a house with a door that locks
and you've got a key to your safety-box
you've got some dignity.
When you own a porch and a garden wall
and friends like Partington and McFaul
you're being pretty wise.
For when you sit you can pick and choose
and it's so much easier on the shoes
than too much exercise.

When a lady has a piazza she has a prize indeed.
She can look on her piazza as a friend in need.
For a girl who has a piazza has a place on which to sit,
and people know a piazza has a house attached to it.

CATALOGUE WOMAN

When I was young and pretty I never could decide
which feller was the feller I would marry.
But when I come to thirty and still was not a bride
my daddy got a little arbitrary.
He took things into his own hands without consulting me,
though Mammy dear almost had a coniption!
He sent my picture to a matrimonial agency
along with a flattering description.

Catalogue Woman, that's how they know me
out in Missouri and Oklahomy,
and there's lots worse things a girl can be
than a catalogue woman.

Right soon there came a letter a-written mighty fine
from a feller with a farm out in Missouri.
He sounded so much better than any friend of mine.
I couldn't think 'twas all quite hunkydory.
He had a thousand acres, and chickens, sheep and cows;
what he needed was a woman on the place.
He 'lowed as how he'd like a girl like me to be his spouse
and how he'd like to meet me face to face.

Catalogue Woman, that's how they know me
out in Missouri and Oklahomy.
There's lots worse things a girl can be
than a catalogue woman.

Well, I went out to Missouri and found the man who'd wrote—
He was even bigger than the letter stated.
He was big and strong as fury, and the heart beneath his coat
was solid gold—it wasn't even plated.

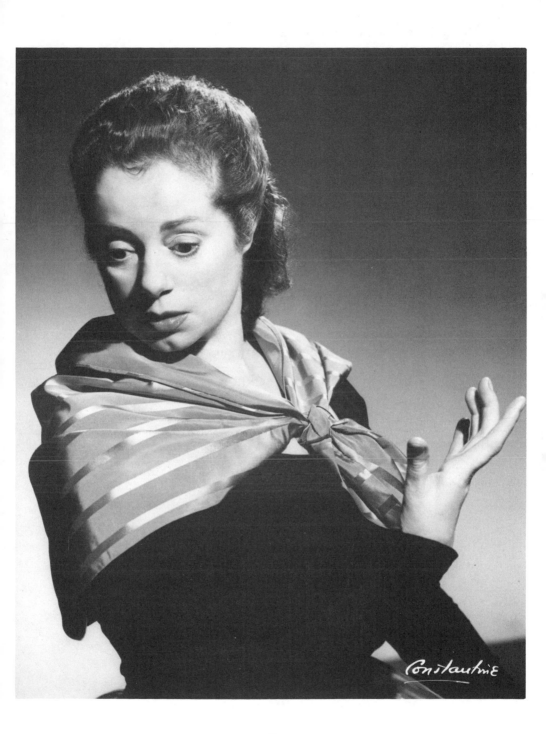

He said I was as welcome as a rainbow in a fog,
and he made it known I wasn't to be taunted.
He said that he was proud he got me from a catalogue—
that way a man could order what he wanted.

Catalogue Woman, that's how they know me
out in Missouri and Oklahomy.
But there's lots worse things a girl can be
than a catalogue woman.

So now I've got a carriage, and hanging on the line
are seven cotton petticoats each Monday.
There couldn't be a marriage any happier than mine,
and Preacher comes to dine most every Sunday.
And if sometimes at Sewing Circle ladies congregate
and whisper things in back of the portières,
I manage to get in a light where I can agitate
the diamonds that are hanging in my ears.

Catalogue Woman, that's how they know me
here in Missouri and Oklahomy.
There's lots worse things a girl can be
than a catalogue woman.

MRS. BADGER-BUTTS

When first I went to work for Mr. Albert Badger-Butts
I hadn't no ulterior ambition.
You couldn't say 'twas my fault Mr. Albert Badger-Butts
was soon in quite a ticklish position.
He'd follow me around all day, and when I'd go to dust
why there'd be Mr. Badger-Butts a-hid behind a bust.
When he'd say "Would I?" I'd say "No," and he'd reply "You must!"
But I wouldn't, so he couldn't, and he fussed and fussed and fussed
till at last I said "Of course, sir, you could marry me, you know!"
He scratched his head and looked at me and said "By Goom,
    that's so!"

Since Mr. Badger-Butts gave me his hyphen
I've never, never, never been the same.
For I've found that when a lady has a hyphen
it changes more than just her name.
As Emmalina Pickett I was nothing
But as Emmalina Badger-Butts, Ah me!
my social standing's risen
till it almost equals his'n
since Mr. Badger-Butts gave me his hyphen.

Now all the tradesmen bow to Mrs. Albert Badger-Butts—
I'm quite the lady when I go to market.
And Bodenheim, the butcher, gives me all his choicest cuts—
I wear my husband's first wife's golden locket.
And every afternoon at four I have my pot of tea,
and it's amazing how the ladies all drop in on me!
The Mayor's wife, the Vicar's wife—it's cozy as can be!
I've got so I can balance now three biscuits on one knee.
At five they all shake hands and go, and when the hall door shuts
who tiptoes up behind me then but Mr. Badger-Butts!

Since Mr. Badger-Butts gave me his hyphen
I've never, never, never been the same.
For I've found that when a lady has a hyphen
it changes more than just her name.
As Emmalina Pickett I was nothing
But as Emmalina Badger-Butts, Ah me!
my social standing's risen
till it almost equals his'n
since Mr. Badger-Butts gave me his hyphen.

I might have picked me out a younger husband, I suppose,
if I'd have had a complete choice in the matter;
but as my mother told me, Mr. Badger-Butts, dear knows,
was practically served on a silver platter.
As she says, "Emmaline, my girl, you mustn't be a chump.
You made it from the pantry to the parlor in one jump.
You've got a horse and carriage, you've got a wedding ring,
and you ought to realize, my girl, you can't have everything!"
And so I just remind myself, when I get aggravated,
whatever other things he lacks, at least he's hyphenated!

Since Mr. Badger-Butts gave me his hyphen
I've never, never, never been the same.
For I've found that when a lady has a hyphen
it changes more than just her name.
As Emmalina Pickett I was nothing
But as Emmalina Badger-Butts, Ah me!
my social standing's risen
till it almost equals his'n
since Mr. Badger-Butts gave me his hyphen!

AT THE LAUNDROMAT

Some ladies join the Junior League—
they think they are right in style,
the Tuesday Club or the Browning Club,
but I got 'em beat a mile.
For I get my dissipation
in a wonderful organization.

At the Laundromat, at the Laundromat,
that's where you'd generally find me at.
When those undies go 'round with a swish and a swirl
it's lots more excitin' than Milton Berle.
So I say, why sit in your flat?
It's more fun at the Laundromat.

What I've found out since I've been there
I'm gettin' quite a file on:
Who's wearin' cotton underwear
and who's wearing silk and nylon.
I find it all very surprisin'
how it broadens your social horizon.

At the Laundromat, at the Laundromat,
that's where you'll generally find me at.
You really get wise to the state of affairs
when you sit there and wait in them chromium chairs.
It's such a fine place for a chat,
that wonderful Laundromat.

One of the customers I meet
Fridays at half-past-ten
is Timothy Blake, the foundry man,
who brings in his washin' then.

I must say it gives me the horrors,
them terrible holes in his drawers!

At the Laundromat, at the Laundromat,
that's where you'll generally find me at.
I told him I wouldn't mind mendin' his pants,
and now we're embarked on a fine romance.
He spends half his time at my flat
when he's not at the Laundromat.

Timothy's an impulsive man.
We washed together twice
when he up and says he'll marry me
and I of course says "That's nice!"
Some women I guess are just gluttons
for men who keep poppin' off buttons.

At the Laundromat, at the Laundromat,
that's where we're holdin' our weddin' at.
It's goin' to be so sanitary and nice
with folks throwin' soap flakes instead of rice
as they follow us back to the flat
from that wonderful Laundromat!

LACKADAISY MASIE

The lady named Masie lived all alone
in a ramshackle house by the river.
She lived in a world that was all her own,
and the village could never forgive her.
If she wanted to sweep by the light of the moon
she took her broom and swept;
if she wanted to stay in her bed till noon
she lay in her bed and slept.
Her lamp would often burn till dawn,
as all her neighbors saw,
and if anybody wondered why her shades weren't drawn,
why there weren't any shades to draw.

Lackadaisy Masie everybody called her.
I guess she must have had another name,
but memories were hazy when it came to Masie,
so Lackadaisy Masie she became.

Masie, people said, had no friends at all—
a thing nobody could pardon—
except for the mice that scurried in her wall
and the squirrels in her tangled garden.
But every few weeks when the tinker came through
in his wagon of yellow and red
he would tether his horse to her chinaberry tree
and pull his cart in her shed.
And all through the night there would be no light
through Masie's windowpane,
but when it was dawn the van would be gone
and out on the roads again.

Lackadaisy Masie, she was like a creeper
that seemed to blossom better in the shade.
If people called her crazy it didn't bother Masie,
so Lackadaisy Masie she stayed.

The tinker he was a dashing man,
flashing his smile so splendid.
The women would flock around his van
and buy what they'd never intended.
Yesterday the tinker arrived in a van
that was shiny and bright and new
and much too big for a single man,
though possibly right for two.
This morning her sagging doors gaped wide,
and when small boys tiptoed there
there was nothing but cobwebs left inside
and Masie's house was bare.

Lackadaisy Masie, she was like an Arab—
a house to her was just a place to stay.
She's found a new oasis, so Lackadaisy Masie's
folded up her tent and gone away.

But there's one thing you can swear to—
they may wander where they care to,
but she'll still be lackadaisy, lackaday!
Lackadaisy Masie—women didn't trust her,
but sometimes when the tinker comes that way
they sigh—and buy a garter
and wonder who was smarter—
Lackadaisy Masie—or they?

THE JANITOR'S BOY

Mother's so busy with clubs and committees
she's gone every morning by nine.
She settles the juvenile problems in cities,
and leaves me to look after mine.
Our housekeeper, Emily, left without notice
and went to seek other employ,
so every day when Mama goes away
I play with the janitor's boy.

O, the janitor's boy isn't handsome;
he's freckled, and thin as a lath,
but he boosted me up on the transom
of Mr. O'Mulvany's bath.
He isn't well-liked by the tenants—
they don't understand him, you see,
but the things that I've done with the janitor's son
have made a new woman of me.

When we play house in the janitor's garret
I'm Mama and he is the Pop.
We quarrel, and I scream just like old Mrs. Barrett
while he beats me up with the mop.
Last week Mr. Jones got a splendid assortment
of Scotch, and two cases of gin.
And did we have fun in the Jones's apartment,
at least till the Joneses walked in!

O the janitor's boy is a marvel,
though not such a popular kid.
He swiped such a funny French novel
that Mrs. Carducci had hid.

Some parts of that book were beyond me—
it was funny the way they would act!
But the janitor's boy made the reading a joy—
he supplied all the knowledge I lacked!

I guess some of the tenants have been pretty stuffy
'bout some of our innocent gags,
like the time we sent cards out that Mrs. McDuffy
was buying up bottles and rags.
I used to sit reading the Sunday School papers
when Mother and Emily were here,
but now I've found out that annoying the neighbors
is really a nicer career!

O, the janitor's boy is my hero—
just think of the games he's contrived!
Like the wonderful day he played Nero
and all of the fire trucks arrived!
The neighbors all think I'm a menace—
they didn't like Nero or Rome.
The juvenile problem they think wouldn't trouble 'em
half so much if Mama stayed at home!

FAITH, HOPE, AND CHARITY

There were three sisters, Faith, Hope, and Charity—
the pride of the town were they,
and they grew up with singular disparity,
each in her own sweet way.
Faith was a good girl, got herself religion,
and Hope started out to roam,
but Charity was contented because
Charity begins at home.

O Charity began at home;
she didn't care to pray or roam.
You'd have never believed
what Charity achieved
when Charity began at home!

There were three sisters, Faith, Hope, and Charity—
O what a fate was theirs!
Faith viewed the other two with critical asperity
and mentioned them in her prayers.
Hope springs eternal, you may have read
in some poetical tome;
Well, Hope would spring at almost any thing
but Charity began at home.

O Charity began at home;
she didn't care to pray or roam.
She figured by remaining
she could do some entertaining,
so Charity began at home.

There were three sisters, Faith, Hope, and Charity:
they created quite a stir,
for Charity saw with singular clarity

her sisters' ways were not for her.
So she stayed home and she cooked and she dusted
and kept things neat as a pin,
and while Faith kept praying and Hope kept straying
Charity just cashed in.

O Charity began at home;
she didn't care to pray or roam.
She'd do better, she was certain,
in behind her parlor curtain,
so Charity began at home.

It wasn't long till her generosity
brought her suitors by the score,
and those who came from pure curiosity
always came back for more.
Her rolls and her muffins were hot from the oven,
her pies drove admirers wild,
and 'twas rumored her Brown Betty had made many a
    man forget 'e
ever had a wife or child.

O Charity began at home,
she didn't care to pray or roam.
In the struggle for survival
Faith and Hope could never rival
what Charity began at home!

THREE LIGHT LADIES

Three light ladies walking in the dew,
along came a soldier and then there were two.
Two light ladies stroll at set of sun,
along came a sailor, and now there is one.
One light lady, sitting all alone
with a dream, and a lamp that murkily shone.
One gray shadow slips across the lawn
and the lamp goes out and the dream comes in
and the last light lady is gone.

Her fingers were made for clinging,
her hair for velvet bows;
her wrist was made for bringing
a rosebud to her nose.
Her lips were made for laughter,
her eyes for easy tears
and her ears were made for the serenade
a lady seldom hears.
Her sisters followed other ways,
and different ways they were,
through thorn and briar and lost desire—
their ways were not for her.
For something deep inside her
kept whispering clear and plain
that her heart was made for waiting
and waiting not in vain.
Alas, the fading darkness,
the hint of dawn, alas!
The swift reluctant footsteps
across the dewy grass.

One light lady in the morning blue,
along went the soldier, and now there are two.
Two light ladies take their morning tea—
along goes the sailor, and now there are three.
Three light ladies face an empty day
with yawns they must hide, and little to say.
One light lady says "Men are such sheep!"
And the second says "Oh?" and the third says "No!"—
and the three light ladies go to sleep;
and the three light ladies - go - to - sleep.

LADY IN WAITING

I am lady-in-waiting to the Queen
Josephine, Josephine,
but of course one's first allegiance must be for
the Emperor, the Emperor.
I cater to her majesty's every whim,
but sometimes when she's indisposed it's pleasant serving him—
one can't always be waiting for the Queen.
Josephine, Josephine.

The Emperor Napoleon doesn't always wear a hat,
and he doesn't always stand with his hand like that;
and when he doffs his tricorne and says he wants the Queen
somebody better run for Josephine!
There are moments when deciding whom and when and
    how to tax
get so arduous an Emperor feels he must relax.
That's when he snaps his fingers for a royal go-between
to run and fetch the Queen.
But if the Queen is occupied with matters of her own,
embroidery, or lessons on the flute,
it isn't fair the Emperor should be left alone
without a substitute!
So when His Majesty beckons and Her Majesty can't come
the lady-in-waiting sallies forth without the roll of drum
and does her humble best to keep Her Majesty's memory green
when she's lady-in-waiting to the Queen.

I am lady-in-waiting to the Queen
Josephine, Josephine.
But of course one's first allegiance must be for
the Emperor, the Emperor.

And so I shut my eyes and murmur "Vive la France!"
and sometimes even "Honi soit que mal y pense!"
One can't always be waiting for the Queen,
Josephine, Josephine.

One time the Empress Josephine went visiting to Madrid
and I wonder if I should have done just as I did?
For when the King suggested that I remain at court
I told him I'd do nothing of the sort.
But sometimes one's allegiances get sadly out of joint
and she can't decide whom she should please, or disappoint.
I thought the matter over, overnight, and changed my mind
and so I stayed behind.
Historians praise the Emperor's skill in military art—
his strategies and tactics in the war,
but I'll record in my memoirs of Bonaparte
the Battle of Boudoir!
I found myself surrounded, out-manoeuvred, and out-flanked,
but I wasn't, it is only fair to mention here, un-thanked.
And after all it's no disgrace, for few have ever won
a battle against Napoleon!

I am lady in-waiting to the Queen,
Josephine, Josephine.
But of course one's first allegiance must be for
the Emperor, the Emperor.
The Queen must realize I'm sure the most important thing
is doing everything one can to save the King—
so if I save His Majesty, God save the Queen
Josephine, Josephine!

DELPHINIA

Delphinia Mack is a widow,
but she has no tear in her eye,
for Delphinia Mack looks very well in black,
as nobody can deny.
Delphinia Mack's been a widow
for only a very few days,
but widowhood has done her good,
everybody says.

As a husband Mack was a drab one,
though of money he had no lack.
Folks wondered, if she had to grab one,
why she ever picked on Mack.
But Delphinia had her reasons,
as some folks claim they knew.
She had no doubt just what she was about
the day she said "I do."

Nobody knew where Delphinia came from,
and nobody stopped to think.
She was suddenly there in the house on the square
with her maid, her Matisse and her mink.
You might perhaps say that the town took Delphinia,
you might say that she took the town,
but whatever you said, she was seasons ahead
when it came to the cut of a gown.

Everyone knew that her clothes came from Paris;
that she never went shopping at Sears.
And six out of seven said her smile came from heaven;
though the seventh had other ideas.

Her charge accounts ran into thousands,
and when creditors came to her door
she'd give them that smile, and they'd wait for a while—
then they'd wait—and they'd wait some more.

Everyone said it was much too good to last,
and wondered when things would crack,
and then one morning, without a word of warning,
she married Oliver Mack.
The town was flabbergasted—they couldn't understand;
they thought her a little bit mad.
They could only believe she had something up her sleeve,
as undoubtedly she had.

For only six weeks later, poor Mack gave up the ghost.
Delphinia got the whole estate.
The undertaker swears, as she led him down the stairs
and let him out the gate
he heard Delphinia murmur, before she turned away—
although of course he could be wrong—
"How nice of Mr. Mack to put me in the black
when I'vc been in the red so long!—
when I've been in the red so long!"

Nobody knows where Delphinia's gone to,
though everyone tries to guess.
But she's no longer there in her house on the square
and she seems to have left no address.
It's true that the postmaster claims that he saw her
the last time he went to New York.
She was done up in pink, and having a drink
with a couple of men at the Stork.

He swears he heard her murmur across her Dubonnet,
although of course he could be wrong—
"How nice of Mr. Fink to fancy me in pink
when I've been wearing black so long, so long—
when I've been wearing black so long!"

THE WIDOW'S WALK

When Abigail Lee walked the Widow's Walk
in her best brocaded gown
she must have known how the widows would talk
all over Portsmouth town.
But she tossed her head, did Abigail Lee,
and turned her glass to the rim of the sea
to look for the sail of the "Hiram Lee"—
or could it have been the "Abbie B"?—
with lips like blood and cheeks like chalk
as she walked her Widow's Walk.

Abigail Barbour was seventeen,
the cobbler's only daughter,
and Hiram Lee, at fifty-three,
had only one love from the day that he
set food on a clipper and put to sea,
and his love of the briny water.

Hiram put on his broadcloth coat
when he came a-courting Abbie.
His face was long as Boston Bay,
and his beard had more than a hint of gray,
but his gold and his clippers seemed to say
that she'd never again go shabby.

The house he built her stood high and tall
to the pride of Abigail Barbour,
and the Widow's Walk on the slated roof
topped all of Portsmouth as though in proof
that Hiram's lady, erect, aloof,
was Queen of Portsmouth Harbor.

Hiram had scoured the seven seas
to prove his love for Abbie;
silks from China and shawls from Spain,
a Persian robe with a peacock train,
a marmoset on a silver chain
and a parrot that spoke Punjabi.

But Abigail paced her Turkey rugs
and found life far from heaven,
for she was alone from sun to sun
and with fourteen years of her marriage done
Abigail Lee was thirty-one
and Hiram was sixty-seven.

Hiram, he skippered the "Hiram Lee,"
but he hired another skipper
to captain his new ship, the "Abbie B,"
a dark and devlish Portygee
with a ring in his ear and a manner free
and bold as a Yankee clipper.

O the Widow's Walk, the Widow's Walk
a bitter walk may prove
when it binds you to a man you hate
and bans a man you love.

Hiram put out on the ninth of June.
but the Portygee waited till summer,
and what occurred in the days between
to credit, folks said, you must have seen,
for things were not as they should have been
'twixt her and that bold new-comer.

What does she wait for, Abigail Lee,
in the chill winds of October?

To and fro on her Widow's Walk
she paces and peers, while people talk,
with lips like blood and cheeks like chalk
in a gown so fine and sober?

She watched in vain, for neither ship
came over the gray horizon.
For Hiram went down in the China Sea
and an iceberg did for the "Abbie B"
and the bones of the swarthy Portygee
are white as the sands he lies on.

O the Widow's Walk, the Widow's Walk
a bitter walk may be
when only the sun and the swinging stars
come over the rim of the sea.

Later when Abigail sent for men as her shipyards
    might require 'em
you'd never have guessed, so Portsmouth says,
that a Portygee with his willful ways
had led her through heaven for fourteen days
after fourteen years of Hiram.
And still sometimes when the winds are high
to her Widow's Walk climbs she.
As she turns her glass through the spray a-blow
who is so wise as to hope to know
if things had been better thus or so
for the widow of Hiram Lee?

O the Widow's Walk, the Widow's Walk
a different walk may be
for the wife of a Yankee sailor man
and the girl of a Portygee.

THE NIGHT OF THE BUTLERS' BALL

Oh the night of the Butlers' Ball
is a wonderful night for us all.
You never would dream, I am sure, by our looks
that we're housekeepers, parlor maids, tweenies and cooks:
we're all Cinderellas right out of the books
on the night of the Butlers' Ball.

Maggie is wearing the mistress's strapless—
it's loose where it ought to be tight.
And she has loaned Nellie an Old Schiaparelli,
and me—I'm a vision in white.
William has borrowed the master's tuxedo
and Jameson is wearing his tails,
and Mrs. O'Hara's got a rhinestone tiara
and one of those polkadot veils.
It's the one night we primp and we perk for
and act like the folks that we work for.

Oh the night of the Butlers' Ball—
on those little gold chairs by the wall
we know how to manage champagne and hors d'oeuvres.
If Emily Post were there she would observe
that we act quite as good as the people we serve
on the night of the Butlers' Ball.

Maggie discovers her strapless is slipping—
she's fearing, I fancy, the worst.
And Nellie is feeling as high as the ceiling—
she's such an unquenchable thirst!
Jameson and William are both looking daggers
at Mrs. Fitzgerald's chauffeur.

It seems they're all took with the Pattersons' cook,
though Lord knows what they see in her!
Is that rhumba she's taking a fling at?
Gracious! Who's William taking a swing at?

Oh the night of the Butler's Ball,
it's a wonderful night for us all.
When the Buffingtons' houseboy got into a fight
with Miss Appleton's footman, and kicked out the light,
it looked just like Ciro's on Saturday night
on the night of the Butlers' Ball.

The men look exactly like Men of Distinction—
and O that divine new valet!
His name is Marcel and he's such a nice smell,
and his voice is just like Charles Boyer!
We danced and we danced till my head was quite dizzy—
I didn't get home until four.
And my room, I confess, when I came to undress,
never looked quite so shabby before.
Still, a girl can't spend all her life caperin'—
tomorrow it's cap and white apron.

O the night of the Butlers' Ball—
what a wonderful night to recall!
Still, thinking about it, I'm a son-of-a-gun
if it don't seem the part that was really most fun
was kicking my shoes off when the whole thing was done
on the night of the Butlers' Ball.

THE YASHMAK

In the heart of Cairo, hid from vulgar gaze,
stands a lovely maid in the bazaar,
and she causes pyro-technical displays
in the hearts of travelers near and far.
Legends of her pallor fill the old Kasbah—
stories of her beauty thrill the town.
But it's only Allah and her own Papa
who've ever seen her with her yashmak down.
And through the oriental night you'll hear
her silvery voice lamenting sweet and clear . . .

If you look behind my yashmak
you will find a gentle dove,
but you can't look there for cash, Mac,
you can only look for love.
Love cannot be bought by barter—
to attempt it is a sin—
for the yashmak hides the daughter
of a single Bedouin.

One night came an Arab—a romantic Sheik—
stealthily the harem wall he scaled.
Brought an emerald scarab—planned to take a peek—
thought that he'd succeed where others failed.
But she heard him coming in the nick of time
and she seized her yashmak from its hook.
So he found her humming her familiar rhyme
while with wild frustration there he shook!
"Oh sir," she cried, "your plotting's of no use.
Oh go and hide your shame in your burnoose!"

If you look behind my yashmak
you will find a gentle dove,
but you can't look there for cash, Mac,
you can only look for love.
Though your heart be young and rash, mac,
ponder well the thing you do!
For if you should take my yashmak
you will have to take me too!

Finally her father said to her "My dear
possibly you'll take a tip from me.
Never raise your yashmak and I rather fear
you will never raise a family."
"Though my heart belongs to Daddy," she replied,
"I'm afraid it's too late to begin.
I shall never have a husband by my side—
never be a double Bedouin!"
So nightly from her lonely minaret
she sings the song no Arab can forget . . .

If you look behind my yashmak
you will find a gentle dove,
But you can't look there for cash, Mac,
you can only look for love!
Take my jewels and take my sash, Mac—
you may have them as a gift.
But if you should lift my yashmak
it's the last you'll ever lift!

ELSA LANCHESTER, born in London, began her long and distinguished career there operating her own intimate night club. Here she met and married Charles Laughton, with whom she appeared in such film classics as *Henry VIII, Rembrandt,* and *The Beachcomber.* The Laughtons came to Hollywood in the '30s where both appeared in many memorable films. In 1941, Elsa joined *Turnabout Theatre,* performing dozens of songs written for her by Forman Brown, becoming, as Charles called her, truly an American *diseuse.* She was at work on this selection of those songs at the time of her death in 1985.

FORMAN BROWN's writing career began with a college musical at the University of Michigan, in 1922. Since then he has written hundreds of songs and sketches for many diverse performers, and lyrics both for Broadway and for several productions of the Los Angeles and San Francisco Light Opera Associations. As co-founder of Turnabout Theatre he was responsible for all the material performed there during the fifteen years of its existence. His published works include poetry, plays, a novel, and two books of reminiscences.